No Spitting Watermelon Seeds

Written by
Martha Rose Woodward

Dedication: To my three children: Barrett, Erin, and Ashley.
Love you more than stars in the sky.

ISBN-13: 978-1477602713 (CreateSpace-Assigned)
ISBN-10: 1477602712

Children's book--non-fiction, gardening, food production, fruits, watermelon, Watermelon Promotion Board, watermelon festival in Cordele, GA, Watermelon Days Festival, watermelon growing, Butler Farm in Blount County, TN, watermelon spitting, watermelon recipes, watermelon lesson plans, Martha Rose Woodward, Knoxville's Sunsphere, Martha Woodward, Knoxville Journal Newspaper, Martha Sunsphere, MarthaSunsphere.blogspot.com, Eva Whitson, Emily Whitson

Manufactured in the United States of America.

Watermelon begins as tiny, black seeds planted in the ground.

Sunshine, water and time to develop must be found.

Small plants push through the soil as they enter the world,

Soon stems and leaves turn into vines that crawl and twirl.

Farmers watch the plants closely for birds and weeds.

Each flower becomes a melon that will produce hundreds of seeds.

The winding vines get longer and larger as they continue to expand.

Next, buds form that burst forth as yellow flowers in this melon-making clan.

The growing cycle of flowers to melons is marvelous to watch indeed, but there is one rule you must always follow, "No spitting watermelon seeds."

A watermelon can be a boy.

A watermelon can be a girl.

That is how reproduction works all over the world.

Bats, birds and bees carry pollen from one flower to another.

The daddy flower must be joined with the flower that is the mother.

Baby melons soon form and farmers pull the weeds,

But remember the rule, there is absolutely

"No spitting watermelon seeds!"

Colors are dark green, light green solid or striped.

Round, oval or oblong, all shapes are well-liked.

Sizes are small, medium, large or extreme, indeed.

No matter color or size, "No spitting watermelon seeds."

Cut a watermelon with a knife and hear it split like a zipper unzipping.

Bite into the pure, seedless heart of a delicious watermelon.

Feel the juice as it oozes over your chin.

You will get energy so you can run, jump and spin.

This is pure summer fun and will meet all your needs,

but remember, "No spitting watermelon seeds."

Watermelon is a fruit. Funny thing but true, watermelon is a vegetable, too.

A fruit will be the contents from a sweet, ripened ovary.

A vegetable is food made or obtained from plants, like a tree.

Watermelon has a family just like you and me.

The name is pronounced ker-kur-bih-TAY-see-ee (cucurbitaceae).

Learn new things, and obey the rule indeed,

Absolutely, "No spitting watermelon seeds."

Cucumbers, squashes, gourds and pumpkins are kind of like cousins.

They grow from little, yellow flowers on vines by the dozens.

But, no matter how you grow them or eat them or the size or color,

you must remember this rule that came from your mother.

To enjoy watermelon when you eat it, you only can succeed

When you do what mother tells you, "No spitting watermelon seeds!"

Parents, grandparents, teachers, big sisters and big brothers, chime in and

Say the same thing as mothers,

"Eat the pink ones, the red, the yellow, even white.

Eat the flesh and the rind fresh, morning, noon, or night."

Use left over parts like the rind and skin for animal feed,

But remember, absolutely, "No spitting watermelon seeds!"

Decorations, pillows, candles, dishes, dresses and shirts.

Are crafted for beauty by millions of experts.

The colors are lively, the fashions are fun.

Clearly there is something beautiful for everyone.

Keep the rule you have learned in order to succeed.

For watermelon real or imagined, "No spitting watermelon seeds!"

California, Arizona, Texas, Georgia and Florida are the top 5 producers.

Men, women, boys, girls, young and old ones are the users.

Farmers say, "We plant them and grow them big to sell to you."

People say, "We love the taste, enjoy the crunch, both at home or at school."

Farmers say, "We pledge ourselves to do our best to accomplish the deed."

Be polite, show your manners, "No spitting watermelon seeds!"

China, Turkey, Iran, Brazil, and the USA are the world's

top growing places.

Japan, Egypt, Mexico also make people have happy faces.

With billions of folks to feed, the fruit is needed by the tons.

Farmers work day and night to feed the daughters and the sons.

No matter where watermelon grows or the customs or the recipes.

People across the globe agree, to be polite there can be, "No spitting

watermelon seeds."

When June arrives and schools are out, kids are ready for some fun.

Time to travel to the beach or mountains for a long vacation.

How about Florida or Tennessee? You say you need a place that's new.

Okay, try Atlanta or Savannah near the ocean where the water is wavy and blue.

Travel makes kids hungry so pick up the speed.

But the rule says there is, "No spitting watermelon seeds!"

Okay, this is the state of Georgia and the name of this city is Cordele.

It's the "Watermelon Capital of the World," and Cordele rhymes with bell.

Each year growing watermelon is celebrated with lots of things to do.

Something for parents, grandparents, teenagers, and little kids, too.

Rumors are going around that something here may be odd.

There is a sign about a contest in the very next yard.

The sign says, "Watermelon Seed Spitting Contest."

Looks like you can spit seeds and beat the rest.

After doing your best to follow the rule,

Can a contest for seed spitting really be true?

Yes, get in line, get ready, time to concede.

You finally have permission to spit watermelon seeds.

The End

Section 2

Butler Farm Blount County, TN

1. Letter to parents and teachers.
2. Lesson plans
3. Contact information
4. Bibliography
5. Comments

Dear Teachers and Parents,

The following lesson plans were written by me and used for many years when I was a classroom teacher. These particular plans were used with students ages 2nd grade through 8th, but would benefit high school level students, too.

I am providing these plans in order for you to use them with your students. The skills taught are listed at the beginning of each plan.

Regards and happy teaching.

Lesson Plans Using Watermelon

Lesson #1

Math-Problem solving

Time needed: 45 minutes to 1 hour   Grade levels: 4 through high school

This lesson involves several steps and can be modified for an entire class or used with small groups of students of all ages. An entire class can complete the lesson with one melon or small groups of 3 to 6 students can use a melon each.

Objectives: The student will use the math skills of problem solving, addition, estimation, subtraction, fractions, drawing conclusions, predicting outcomes, finding mean, median, and mode, determining the weight of an object in pounds and ounces using scales, recording data on charts, larger than/less than, and writing questions.

Materials needed: One whole watermelon or one melon per group of students, paper/pencil/markers, charts, scales, towels, plastic knives, napkins

Directions: Ask students what it means to guess. Introduce the word "estimation" and give the meaning as guessing. Give each student a small piece of paper and ask them to write his/her name on the paper. Next, show the melon and ask each student to write his/her guess as to how much the melon weighs on the paper. Take the papers up and write their guesses beside their names on a large chart or on a display board. Ask who made the largest guess? The smallest? Use other questions as you think of them.

Have the students to add the total for all guesses; find the average. Teach the concepts of mean; median and mode.

Weigh the melon. Check to see if the exact weight was guessed. Ask students whose guess was the closest and least closest. Ask the students to ask some questions about the estimation of the weight of a melon. Did most students guess nearest to the correct weight? Do melons weigh less or more than they look like they could? Ask the students how many parts you have if you cut the melon into half? Cut the melon and keep asking about fractional parts. Have students to write or ask math questions about the lesson.

End the lesson by allowing the students to eat the melon.

Lesson #2 Fractions--halves/ fourths/eighths
Objectives: The students will use watermelon to explore math and reading skills.
Students will read directions, determine sequence, determine cause and effect, and
discuss the results of an activity.

In order for students to learn the most from Lesson #2, they need to complete Lesson #1.

Materials needed:
A watermelon (WITH SEEDS) for the entire class or one per group of 3 to 6 students.
Towels and napkins
Paper/pencil/markers/crayons
Class charts and board space

Directions: Using one whole watermelon, the teacher will ask the students to predict how
many pieces will result if she/he cuts the melon one time in equal parts. The teacher
writes 1/2 on the board and also 2/2 while discussing. Next, ask how many pieces result
when the 1/2 sections are cut into equal parts. ¼ + ¼ . Also write ¾ and 4/4 on the board.

Ask the students to copy and solve ¼ + 2/4 +   ¼+ ¾ = and 2/4 + 2/4= ½+½=

Continue with fourths and eighths until all have mastered these skills.

Lesson #2 continued

Give each student a piece of melon. Ask them to estimate how many seeds they think are in their piece of melon and to write it on paper. Next, tell them to count the number of seeds in their piece of melon and write the total.

Ask each student to share their total with a partner or group of other students. Ask the students to add their totals. Keep going until all are added and there is a class total.

Find the class total, the average, and mean and the mode. Check to see if anyone guessed correctly. Determine who got the closest, etc.

Students may eat the melon, but tell them to save the seeds.

Lesson #3 Artwork using fresh melon and seeds.

Ask students to create a colorful piece of artwork using seeds, crayons, and/or pencil drawings or colleges.

Ask the students, if these were not seeds what might they be if you added lines? Insects, buttons on clothing, eye balls, knobs, etc.

Ask students to share their artwork and to discuss their inspiration; others may ask questions. Use artwork to decorate the classroom.

Wally Watermelon
Mascot for Cordele, Georgia

Watermelon is one of the USA's largest cash crops. Crisp County is Georgia's number 1 watermelon-growing county and the number 4 watermelon-growing county in the United States. The most prominent watermelons grown in Crisp County are seedless, red watermelons. Cordele Georgia is known as the **Watermelon Capital of the World** because of the quality and quantity of watermelons grown in the county. During the summer, Cordele celebrates the watermelon harvest with the annual Watermelon Days Festival that includes parades, fashion shows, watermelon chunking and watermelon decorating contest, watermelon cooking and watermelon eating, as well as a watermelon spitting seed contest. For an entire list of all activities, go to the website for the Cordele, Georgia Chamber of Commerce at www.http://www.cordelecrispga.com/

The National Watermelon Promotion Board or NWPB was formed in 1989 by watermelon growers and shippers to increase consumer demand for watermelon through promotion, research, and educational programs. The Orlando-based non-profit organization seeks to develop marketing programs that boost watermelon sales in supermarkets throughout the United States and Canada.

The NWPB says that watermelon is not just for picnics anymore, but has become a staple on the shopping lists of consumers who enjoy the tasty treat year-round since it is summer somewhere in the world every day. Consumers can learn fun facts, history, recipes and much more from the web site at http://www.watermelon.org

Alabama, Florida, Georgia, Indiana, Maryland-Delaware, North Carolina, South Carolina and Texas each have state associations that promote the sale of watermelon.

Bibliography

The Butler Farm in Blount County, TN
http://www.cordelecrispga.com/
http://www.giantwatermelons.com/
http://www.nationalwatermelonassociation.com/
www.ncmelons.com/
http://ohioline.osu.edu/hyg-fact/1000/1626.html
http://www.watermelon.org/
Watermelon Days Festival
Watermelon Promotion Board
Wikipedia entries for watermelon, Kalahari desert and world map

www.marthasunsphere.blogspot.com

Cordele Chamber of Commerce
302 E. 16th Avenue
Cordele, Georgia 31015

National Watermelon Promotion Board
3361 Rouse Road
Suite 150
Orlando, FL 32817

Woodward's TV Show: Homespun Hobbies
Airs weekly on www.ctvknox.org
(available to watch on-line)

Photos in this book are by Martha Rose Woodward
Child model, Eva Whitson (photos by Emily Whitson)
Many thanks to Donna and James Butler for photos of their farm.

Words You Should Know About Watermelon

1. Pulp 2. Farmer 3. Kalahari Desert 4. Rind 5. Hybrid 6. Harvest 7. Striped
8. Oblong 9. Citrullus lanatus 10. Cultivate

World production of watermelon in metric tons:
1 China 62,256,973
2 Turkey 3,796,680 S
3 Iran 3,300,000
4 Brazil 2,092,630
5 United States 1,944,490
http://www.top5ofanything.com/index.php?h=a134d02f

Comments Page:

What people are saying about *No Spitting Watermelon Seeds,* a new children's book by Martha Rose Woodward.

"Children are our future and this book could not be more timely. It teaches the life cycle of a watermelon and the values of patience, hard work, diligence and more, along with reinforcing reading skills. This book is a must for parents who want their children to start out learning to love books and with strong values."
--Douglas Young- Founder of the Modern Tribune, writer/spokesperson for the Knoxville Journal Newspaper.

"No Spitting Watermelon Seeds teaches us all how simple watermelons, grown from tiny seeds in so many different types of surroundings, can become so many delightfully different things enjoyed by *everyone* all over the world. It teaches us how the right amount of care and nurturing, along with an ample amount of patience, can bring enormous joy and satisfaction."
- Kevin Jeske Director of Development - Community Television of Knoxville

"What a great way to get young students to think about math and science. The kids will love it. So will their teachers. I also like the idea that the subject matter is a healthy food." Terry Shaw, author, "*The Way Life Should Be.*" President of Knoxville Writers' Guild

"Good book. Good illustrations. Congratulations and good luck. Keep going out into the world, Martha, and making it a better place," Russell Devore, M.D. Cancer Specialists of East Tennessee.

Thanks so much for visiting our 5th grade class at Knoxville Christian School. What a treat! Robin Flournoy, teacher

"This book brings me back to my childhood. I'm afraid I broke the rule, because I did spit seeds," Jerry, age 65

"I can't get this out of my mind. So beautiful!" Sandra Lea, author of *Whirlwind: the Butcher Banking Scandal.*

More information about Woodward's Writing Career:
Woodward's television program, Homespun Hobbies, airs on-line each week at
www.ctvknox.org and on TV Channels 6 and 12 in Knoxville, TN.
Read Woodward's blog at www.marthasunsphere.blogspot.com
Read Woodward's articles in The Knoxville Journal Newspaper each week.
Other books by Woodward:

Knoxville's Sunsphere; Biography of a Landmark , a 208 page, nonfiction book, was published in September 2007, by
Video Publishing and Printing, Schaad Road, in Knoxville, Tennessee, Tim Carroll, publisher. The author is Martha Rose
Woodward, a retired school teacher, who turned her creative talents into a part-time career by going to work for a local
newspaper, The Knoxville Journal. Woodward's book uses personification to turn the unique tower which was built as the
theme structure for the 1982 World's Fair, into a person. "The Sunsphere has had an interesting life during the last 26
years and I thought it was a story that needed to be told," said Woodward. With input from the architect who dreamed up
the building, William Denton, former Mayor Randy Tyree, and Jesse Barr, financial advisor to the Sunsphere, Woodward
conducted most of the research for her book at the East Tennessee History Center as well as through personal
interviews. "If anyone has walked in and out of the Sunsphere during the last twenty-five years, Martha has interviewed
them," said William Denton of Woodward's attention to detail.
The book is available for sale at Amazon.com and from the author by e mail at Sunspherebook@aol.com

Knoxville's 1982 World's Fair
From May 1 through October 31, 1982, Knoxville hosted the world's fair based on the theme "Energy Turns the World."
Expo '82 was the first world's fair to be held in the southeastern United States in 97 years, hosting 22 countries and more
than 11 million people. Once referred to as the "scruffy little city by the Tennessee River," Knoxville provided one big party
for people to visit from all over to witness the live entertainment, parades, displays, exhibits, musical and sporting events,
food, costumes, rides, games, and arcades. The news reports of the day declared the "World Came to Knoxville" as it
hosted the official international exposition, fully licensed and sanctioned by the Bureau des Expositions Internationales in
Paris, France. The 128 page Images of America book has become one of the newest of the 3,500 titles produced by
Arcadia Publishing from Mt. Pleasant, South Carolina. To order your copy please visit www.arcadiapublishing.com or e
mail Martha Rose at Sunspherebook@aol.com The price is $22.

Seven Minutes in Hell: the Eric McLean Murder Case
by Martha R. Woodward

"Love Triangle" or "Deadly Teacher-Student Murder Case"--the death of Sean Powell came to the attention of the nation in 2007 when the man who pulled the trigger of a 360 Marlin rifle killed the eighteen year old with one shot to his head. Woodward's research follows the characters in this story through over two years of events. After the murder, a wild-haired man was taken into custody while his wife fled town with her children. The man accused of murder filed for divorce against his cheating spouse.

Next, bizarre tales floated through the community as a young women moved from town to town on the lam with her young children. Eventually, t he shooter faced charges for first degree murder as he squared off in court against a determined District Attorney. In a shocking ending the victim's families watched as the man who killed their child skated through the court system with the lightest of sentences.

Available from the author at Sunspherebook@aol.com . $8

Even Wounded Birds Fly
by Martha R. Woodward

a novel by Martha Rose Woodward

When a group of young boys in rural Alabama become aware of the sexual abuse of their most vulnerable comrade, Milton, they decide to take matters into their own hands. At a time when such matters were not discussed openly, the boys scheme to prevent the town's highly respected preacher from any possibility of furthering Milton 's darkest nightmare.

Are these boys conspiring to commit an act of murder or is the elimination of this spiritual vampire an act of justice? Whatever the truth, the boys decide to bludgeon the preacher and throw his body down an abandoned well. Having also tossed their innocence and youth into that dark pit, they must then live the remainder of their lives burdened with this ghastly secret.

Enter into the picture Rita Belew, a young woman living a fairy-tale marriage until an unexpected revelation shatters her world. The heartbreak of her failed marriage renders her sexually and emotionally vulnerable, and she must somehow fashion a future out of the ashes of this tragedy. It is in this fragile state of mind that she meets Rodney Edgely, a professional speaker who presents himself as a sincere gentleman. However, Rita slowly begins to question the mysterious behaviors of her new companion while struggling to admit what is plainly before her eyes. Could the very person that she should most be able to trust be leading a double life?

Eventually the past, present, and future collide and expose unimaginable secrets and long-buried fears. The explosive combination of shocking lies and shattered egos fuels a showdown where hasty decisions become a matter of life and death. While the colorful characters struggle with their naked pasts and uncertain futures, in the end, their intertwined lives illuminate the deepest meaning of love.

Many thanks to Donna and James Butler for allowing me to visit their farm and make photos of the various stages of the life of the watermelon plants.

What Is an Idiom

When IT'S AT Home?

by Emma Carlson Berne

Consultant: Robert L. McConnell, PhD

Fact Finders Books are published by Capstone Press,
1710 Roe Crest Drive, North Mankato, Minnesota 56003
www.mycapstone.com

Library of Congress Cataloging-in-Publication Data
Cataloging-in-publication information is available on the Library of Congress website.
978-1-5157-6388-8 (library binding)
978-1-5157-6393-2 (paperback)
978-1-5157-6405-2 (ebook PDF)

Editorial Credits:
Michelle Bisson, editor; Bobbie Nuytten, designer; Tracy Cummins, media researcher;
Laura Manthe, production specialist

Photo Credits:
Dreamstime: Ankevanwyk, 22; iStockphoto: Duncan Walker, 14, quisp65, 20;
Shutterstock: Andrey_Kuzmin, cover (right), Aratehortua, 27, BlueRingMedia, 12,
burnel1, cover (bottom), Complot, 10, Dmytro Zinkevych, 25 (bottom), dragon_fang,
24, easyshutter, 16–17, Eric Isselee, cover (middle), Erik Lam, cover (top left), Fabio
Balbi, 26 (top), Guzel Studio, 8, InesBazdar, 15, Kajano, 19, kalenderenk, 9, Ken Cook,
6 (top), kstudija, cover and interior design element, lineartestpilot, 18, mezzotint,
13, Michele Paccione, 6 (bottom), Natykach Nataliia, 21, nikitabuida, 25 (top),
Olga_Angelloz, 4, Rawpixel.com, 5, Rob Hyrons, cover (bottom left), Studio_G, 28;
Wikimedia: National Archives and Records Administration, 26 (bottom)

Printed in China.
010343F17

Table of Contents

CHAPTER ONE

Dressing the Chicken:
What Is an Idiom?

Amelia Bedelia could not understand idioms. This fictional storybook maid "drew the drapes" with a sketchpad and a pencil. Mrs. Rogers, her boss, tells her to dress the chicken for dinner. Amelia Bedelia puts the bird in a little pair of green overalls. All of this makes for very funny fiction. Amelia Bedelia's antics also remind readers that understanding idioms is important. Idioms are useful and widely used.

An idiom is a phrase or a sentence that is a specific to the language and culture of the speaker or writer. A writer who is writing in English in the American South will use certain words or phrases. "I came up with her," she might say, meaning "I was raised with her." A writer writing in British English might use different words or phrases. For instance, Americans say and write "cross the road." British writers might say or write "go over the road." Both are correct, of course, but "go over the road" sounds odd to American ears, just as "cross the road" might sound odd to British ears.

Did You Know?

People often describe someone anxiously waiting as being on tenderhooks. The word is actually tenterhooks, and it comes from the days in which newly made fabric was stretched on a frame, with hooks—tenter-hooks—to dry.

Idioms sometimes, but not always, have a **figurative** meaning instead of a **literal** meaning. "Don't make a mountain out of a molehill" does not mean to create a hill with the piles of dirt that moles leave on your lawn. It means don't make a big deal out of something small. Here's another example: "It's raining cats and dogs." Quick! Does that mean a) dachshunds and Persians are literally falling from the clouds and creating doggy and kitty puddles on the ground? or b) It's raining very hard. If you can't answer that question, you may not be a native speaker of English, in which case you get a free pass.

Another example is a phrase you use when you are out of the house. An American might say he or she is "not at home." But a native Brit might say that he or she is "from home." There is no reason why one should say "at home" versus "from home." It's just the way each of our versions of English have evolved.

Buried Idioms

Often, idioms can be buried in regular sentences. **Phrasal verbs** are idioms as well. These figurative verbs often stump nonnative English speakers. For instance, you might bring the matter up at a business meeting. You're not literally lifting something from the floor. Or a person might be cut out for a particular job. No scissors involved—that person is simply right for the job. Someone who's had a bad experience might bounce back. No jumping, no ricocheting off a surface. Or how about egging someone on? No eggs are actually involved. The phrase means to **goad** someone into doing something—usually something foolish. The list of phrasal verbs is practically infinite, but it's colorful language like this that keeps our writing bright. Often though, phrasal verbs are overused and tired—they become **clichés** and lose some of their effectiveness.

figurative—expressing one thing in terms normally used for another
literal—following the ordinary or usual meaning of the words
phrasal verb—group of words that work as a verb; phrasal verbs can be idioms
goad—to urge something
cliché—phrase or expression that has been used many times

Idioms vs. Clichés

Idioms and clichés are sometimes linked. Clichés can be, and often are, idioms. And some, but not all, idioms are clichés. "Her hair was as black as night," is a clichéd way of describing something very black, for instance.

When used well, idiomatic phrases can add a fresh slant to your writing. "He's as tough as woodpecker lips." Brilliant, right? Fresh and weird. Here's another one: "He was off like a dirty shirt." Idioms can take a specific image and slam it into the reader's brain. They make the reader laugh unexpectedly or blink in surprise. Idioms give writers job security. Robots can't create idioms.

TRY IT OUT!

Write three sentences that include idioms. Then rewrite those sentences, removing the idioms but **retaining** the original meaning.

retain—to keep something

Any nonnative English language learner will tell you that our language, with all of its nonsensical spellings and weird sentence construction, is a headache to learn. And idioms don't make things any easier. There's no rule for them. You have to learn each idiom individually. And you have to get them exactly right. Reversing the words can mark you as a nonnative speaker. Raining dogs and cats? Sounds strange, right? That's because idioms have a certain rhythm and sequence to them, like poetry.

And every language has idioms. "Don't judge a book by its cover" is familiar to native English speakers. In French, a familiar idiom is, "I can do this *les doights dans le nez*," or "fingers in the nose," meaning "I can do this so easily that I can do it with my fingers in my nose." Idioms are hard to translate, and sometimes hard to understand. But they make our writing unique and flavorful. During periods of war, suspected spies posing as Americans have been asked to repeat American idioms as a test. The reasoning: only real Americans would be able to identify idioms from his or her native country.

Idiom vs. Literal Meaning

IDIOM	LITERAL MEANING	IF IDIOMS WERE REAL LIFE
I wouldn't be caught dead.	I would never do that.	I'm in a coffin, hoping to evade capture.
Pull the wool over her eyes.	Fool her.	Get some of this soft, puffy fleece. Now make it into a woolly blindfold, ok?
Elvis has left the building.	The matter is over. Everything has been decided.	Elvis Presley, the dead rock-and-roll singer, is not in this building. In fact, he is in the cemetery.
You hit the nail on the head.	You exactly understand the matter.	Good work with that hammer! You precisely whacked the protruding nail.
Don't cut corners.	Don't do a bad job to save time or money.	Measure out each piece of wood exactly, okay? If it says one inch, you measure and cut one inch.
Back to the drawing board!	Time to start over with new ideas.	Time to return to the large, flat board I use for drawing!
Time to hit the sack!	Time to go to bed!	It's time to take my fist and punch a large cloth bag!

11

CHAPTER TWO

A Stitch in Time:
Idioms and History

Many idioms are examples of figurative language. But they didn't start out this way. They started out as literal words. The phrasing was **succinct**, perhaps. Maybe someone famous said those words, perhaps in a public setting. Maybe it was a particularly clever or poetic way to express an idea. Whatever the reason, the phrase caught on.

For instance, "kicked the bucket" means died, not literally kicking over a mop pail. Where did it come from? Most scholars agree that the phrase comes from the practice of hanging a slaughtered animal, like a pig, upside down from a beam. The beam was called a bucket. An animal might sometimes kick after slaughter— striking the bucket. Over time, the literal meaning disappeared, perhaps as farming became less common, but the colorful phrase or sentence hung on.

The way we use it now, the phrase "white elephant" means a cumbersome gift or possession no one really wants. Originally, it did mean white elephants. In Thai history before the 20th century, white-colored elephants were highly prized. A king might give a white elephant to someone as a sign of that person's worth. English and European writers noticed this custom. They made up a story about it: that giving a white elephant was actually a way to punish someone. The animals were rare and prized, but also expensive to take care of. It wasn't really a gift anyone wanted. And an idiom was born.

succinct—to speak or write clearly without wasted words

Shakespeare's Idioms

The English language's most famous playwright and poet is William Shakespeare. Shakespeare lived in England from 1564 until 1616. Shakespeare is the source of many, many idioms. His poetry and plays were immensely popular and the music and playfulness of his words captivated his audience. It's no surprise that so many of his words have hung on.

Idioms Everywhere

All languages contain idioms. And they're all different. The Germans, for example, say "Tomaten auf den Augen haben." That means, "You have tomatoes on your eyes." It means someone is not seeing what others are seeing. Or if you are in Sweden and you're concerned about a test, your mother might say, "Det är ingen ko på isen," or "there's no cow on the ice." A cow standing on a frozen pond would be very dangerous and serious—the cow could fall through the ice and die. So saying "there's no cow on the ice" means "there's no great emergency." And in France, if you have flunked a test, you might mutter to yourself, "Les carottes sont cuites!" That means, "The carrots have been cooked." In other words, there's no sense in crying over spilt milk.

Maybe you've been in an awkward new social situation. No one really knows each other and no one is talking. You can suggest the group play a game to "break the ice." You probably didn't know you were quoting Shakespeare, but you were! In his play *The Taming of the Shrew*, the character named Tranio talks to a character named Hortensio about a plan to marry a woman:

> *If it be so, sir, that you are the man,*
>
> *Must stead us all, and me amongst the rest,*
>
> *And if you break the ice and do this feat,*
>
> *Achieve the elder, set the younger free*
>
> *For our access, whose hap shall be to have her*
>
> *Will not so graceless be to be ingrate.*

"You're the one who can help us all," Tranio says. "You can start us off on this interaction." In other words, Tranio thinks that Hortensio can "break the ice."

How about "wild-goose chase"? It means a fruitless hunt for something, but did you know the phrase originated in that ultimate love story, *Romeo and Juliet*? That's right. Romeo and his best buddy Mercutio are being silly with each other, bantering back and forth the way guys do, and Mercutio says, "Nay, if our wits run the wild-goose chase, I am done, for thou hast more of the wild-goose in one of thy wits than, I am sure, I have in my whole five. Was I with you there for the goose?" Of course, Mercutio doesn't mean to literally run after a wild, runaway goose. He means that this search is going to be pointless.

Other **iconic** texts have contributed their own fair share of idioms. The Bible gives Shakespeare a run for his money (ding! Idiom related to horse racing!) "Eye for an eye"? "Cross to bear"? "Bite the dust"? That's right—those are all from the Bible. Our iconic texts continue to give our language life and color.

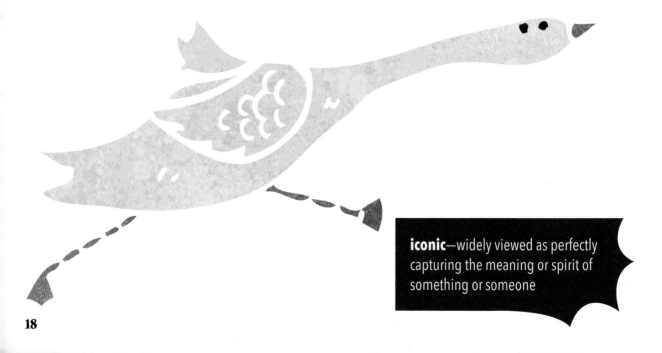

iconic—widely viewed as perfectly capturing the meaning or spirit of something or someone

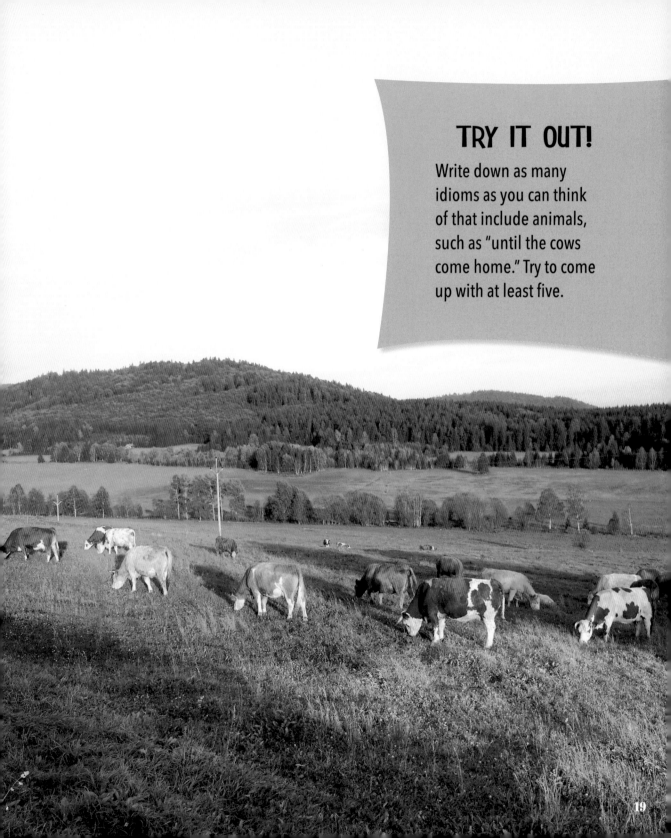

TRY IT OUT!

Write down as many idioms as you can think of that include animals, such as "until the cows come home." Try to come up with at least five.

CHAPTER THREE

Make That Idiom Work for You

So now we know that a cliché is an idiom that's overused. Idioms are often inserted unthinkingly into writing and speech because that's just the way we say certain things. But just because some idioms are comfortable or tired doesn't mean that idioms have no place in your writing. To the contrary, idioms can add color and fun. An idiom can get a big idea across in a few choice words. A strange idiom, like "chew the fat," or a funny idiom, like "when pigs fly," can snag the reader's attention, make him or her laugh out loud, or say an internal, "ahhh, yes!"

TRY IT OUT!

Take these three popular idioms and change them into new idiomatic phrases—extra points for humor and absurdity. For example, "raining cats and dogs" might be changed to "pelting petunias and peacocks."

Her lips were red as a rose.

Take it with a grain of salt.

That's the best thing since sliced bread!

But idioms are like salt—a little bit sprinkled just right adds that little kick of flavor you were missing. Too much salt? Your scrambled eggs are **inedible**. For instance, imagine that you wrote:

> "Gosh, I'm all thumbs today!" Melanie declared, after knocking over her coffee.

> "Maybe you bit off more than you could chew," Darryl commented. "After all, you are trying to do the crossword in pen."

> "You can say that again," Melanie agreed. "You know what? I've got no skin in this game." She pitched the pen out the window. "After all, I always say, in for a penny, in for a pound." And she threw the coffee cup out the window as well.

A Different Version

The story on the previous page is silly. Still, Melanie and Darryl's insistence on piling on idioms makes them sound as if they are brainless. Now, compare what they said before with this version:

"Whoops!" Melanie grabbed for her coffee cup, but it was too late. The brown liquid spread across the table, soaking Darryl's paper.

"Maybe you're trying to do too much, dear," Darryl said, letting his paper drip over the sink. "After all, it would take a braver person than I to do the crossword in pen."

"Oh, Darryl, why are you always right?" Melanie crossed her arms on her chest and scowled. "It kind of makes me hate you a little."

Darryl wisely kept quiet and after a moment, Melanie sighed. "You know what? I'm through torturing myself." She opened up the window and pitched the crossword and the pen into the garden. They landed in the dahlias. Melanie stared at them a moment. "Why not?" she muttered and pitched the coffee cup out too.

This version gets the story across without heavy **reliance** on idioms. It uses other language, such as descriptive words, more precise dialogue, and action verbs, to create pictures in the reader's mind.

inedible—not safe for eating

reliance—dependence on someone or something

CHAPTER FOUR

Idioms Ahead:
The Future's So Bright

"Language is always evolving" is a sort of cliché in itself, but it's also true. We still use all sorts of words from Old English, which was spoken before 1100. Eke (to get the most out of something by using it carefully) or sleight (the use of cunning, as in "sleight of hand") are examples of Old English words that we still use.

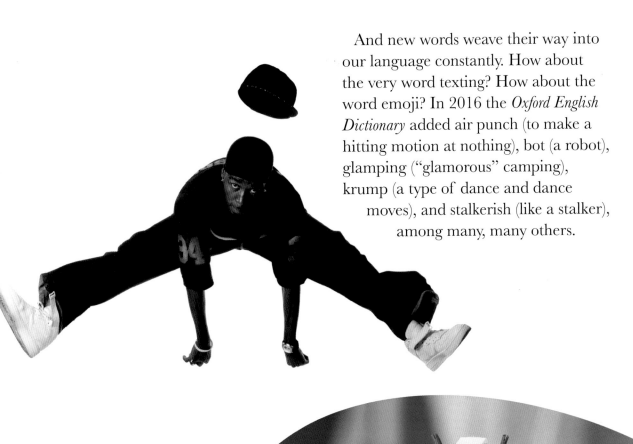

And new words weave their way into our language constantly. How about the very word texting? How about the word emoji? In 2016 the *Oxford English Dictionary* added air punch (to make a hitting motion at nothing), bot (a robot), glamping ("glamorous" camping), krump (a type of dance and dance moves), and stalkerish (like a stalker), among many, many others.

Idioms aren't always composed of words. Punctuation can function as a sort of idiom as well. Have you seen anyone Do. This. Online. Ever? Separating each word with a period to add emphasis to a point is pretty effective. How about putting a picture or a link up on social media and writing simply "THIS."

Did You Know?

Have you heard of committing yourself to something as unpleasant as "biting the bullet"? This idiom once was exactly what it sounds like. On 19th century battlefields, the doctor might give you an actual lead bullet to bite on before he amputated your leg. Bonus fact: You would bite on the bullet so you wouldn't bite off your own tongue!

Emojis as Idioms

EMOJI	LITERAL MEANING
	Love you! Kisses!
	Fist bump! We can do this!
	I'm laughing so hard, I'm crying!
	This is silly, what I'm saying right now.
	I'm pretty embarrassed.
	You're strong, or I'm strong.
	Oh no! I'm scared! or, This is very bad!
	We're together on this, I'm with you.

Idioms vs. Slang

There is a difference, though, between idioms and slang. Slang refers to words that are very casual, and are used in certain situations—such as when you are with your friends. Teachers usually don't allow slang in student writing. They usually do allow idioms. However, certain phrases and emojis can be considered modern idioms. Texting your friend "LOL" is more pithy and sharp than spelling out the entire phrase. When you're furious at your mother, a frowning face emoji on your phone says all you need to say. On the other hand, your mother will probably want a little more explanation!

Sometimes, older people feel anxious about how they think young people are messing up the language. Some people feared the telephone was going to destroy writing. And while it's true that the way we write and speak now is quite different from how our 19th century ancestors did, it's also true that the English language is as alive and rich as it's ever been. We add new words, we discard old ones, we hang onto others—just as we've always done. Idioms show up, they turn into clichés, they fade away, and new ones are created. Hearing new idioms can be exciting, but it's just another sign that our language is alive and evolving.

Glossary

cliché (klee-SHAY)—phrase or expression that has been used many times

figurative (FIG-yur-eh-tiv)—expressing one thing in terms normally used for another

goad (GOHD)—to urge something

iconic (EYE-kon-ik)—widely viewed as perfectly capturing the meaning or spirit of something or someone

inedible (in-ED-eh-buhl)—not safe for eating

literal (LIT-ur-uhl)—following the ordinary or usual meaning of the words

phrasal verbs (FRAZ-uhl VURB)—group of words that work as a verb; phrasal verbs can be idioms

reliance (ri-LYE-anse)—dependence on someone or something

retain (ri-TAYN)—to keep something

succinct (suh-SINKT)—to speak or write clearly without wasted words

Read More

Grammar and Punctuation. Collins Easy Learn. New York: HarperCollins, 2015.

Fielder, Heidi. *The Know-Nonsense Guide to Grammar: An Awesomely Fun Guide to the Way We Use Words!* Know Nonsense Series. Lake Forest, Calif.: Walter Foster Jr., 2017.

Sabra, Ponn, and **Habeeba Husain**. *Poetic Puns: Grammar Made Fun*. Ponn Press, Amazon Digital Services, 2013.

Critical Thinking Questions

1. What is the difference between an idiom and a cliché? Provide an example by using each in a paragraph.

2. This text provides many examples of idioms. How do examples help the reader understand the author's meaning?

3. What is your favorite idiom found in this text? Explain why you like this particular idiom.

Internet Sites

Use FactHound to find Internet sites related to this book.

Visit *www.facthound.com*

Just type in 9781515763888 and go!

 Check out projects, games and lots more at
www.capstonekids.com

Index